The publisher acknowledges the support of the Government of Canada, Department of Canadian Heritage, Book Publishing Industry Development Program.

ISBN 1-55082-300-0

Design by Sari Naworynski.

Printed and bound in Canada by Champlain Graphics, Pickering, Ontario.

Published by Quarry Press Inc., 1180 Medical Court, Suite A, Carmel, Indiana 46032 and 195 Allstate Parkway, Markham, Ontario L3R 4T8.

QUARRY
HERITAGE

BOOKS

America the Beautiful

Lyrics by Katharine Lee Bates

Illustrations by Susan Winget

Sung by Daniel Rodriguez

O beautiful for spacious skies,
For amber waves of grain,

For purple mountain majesties
Above the fruited plain!

O beautiful for spacious skies

America! America!
God shed his grace on thee

And crown thy good with brotherhood
From sea to shining sea!

"sea to shining sea"

O beautiful for pilgrims feet
Whose stern, impassioned stress

A thoroughfare of freedom beat
Across the wilderness!

America! America!
God mend thine every flaw,

Confirm thy soul in self-control,
Thy liberty in law!

O beautiful for heroes proved
In liberating strife,

Who more than self their country loved,
And mercy more than life!

America! America!
May God thy gold refine

Till all success be nobleness
And every gain divine!

O beautiful for patriot dream
That sees beyond the years,

Thine alabaster cities gleam
Undimmed by human tears!

Sweet land of Liberty

America! America!
God shed his grace on thee

And crown thy good with brotherhood
From sea to shining sea!

O beautiful for halcyon skies,
For amber waves of grain,
For purple mountain majesties
Above the enameled plain!

America! America!
God shed his grace on thee
Till souls wax fair as earth and air
And music-hearted sea!

O beautiful for pilgrims feet,
Whose stern, impassioned stress
A thoroughfare for freedom beat
Across the wilderness!

America! America!
God shed his grace on thee
Till paths be wrought through wilds of thought
By pilgrim foot and knee!

O beautiful for glory-tale
Of liberating strife
When once and twice, for man's avail
Men lavished precious life!

America! America!
God shed his grace on thee
Till selfish gain no longer stain
The banner of the free!

O beautiful for patriot dream
That sees beyond the years
Thine alabaster cities gleam
Undimmed by human tears!

America! America!
God shed his grace on thee
Till nobler men keep once again
Thy whiter jubilee!

George Washington
United we
Stand...

THE STORY OF THE SONG

America the Beautiful was written by Katharine Lee Bates. A children's author and an English professor, she was born in the sea-side town of Falmouth, Massachusetts, and taught at Wellesley College. In 1893, Katharine toured the United States, first visiting the Chicago World's Fair and then trekking to the top of Pikes Peak in Colorado. She climbed the peak in a prairie wagon pulled by mules. Her view of the Rocky Mountains and the Great Plains inspired her to write *America the Beautiful*. "When I saw the view," Katharine wrote in her journal, "I felt great joy. All the wonder of America seemed displayed there, with a sea-like expanse." Her sense of wonder is shared by all Americans, from "sea to shining sea."

First published as a poem, Katharine's lyrics were soon set to the music of the familiar hymn *Materna* composed by Samuel A. Ward. *America the Beautiful* has since become a favorite patriotic song and the unofficial second national anthem of the United States, sung wherever Americans gather to celebrate the glory of their country.

For more information about Katharine Lee Bates and *America the Beautiful*, visit her home in Falmouth, Massachusetts or contact the Falmouth Historical Society on the Internet at www.falmouthhistoricalsociety.org.